An Olio of Poems
by Christina J Donato
and Ralph A Walton

All rights reserved. No part of this book may be reproduced, stored in a retrieval system, or transmitted in any form or by any means – electronic, mechanical, photocopy, recording, or otherwise – except for brief quotations for the purpose of review or comment, without the prior permission of the publisher, Left-handed Author Publishing. You can reach them at cjdlefty@gmail.com.

Published in the United States of America by Left-handed Author Publishing, Cranston, RI.

Printed in the United States of America.
"An Olio of Poems"
Copyright © 2025 Christina J Donato

Library of Congress Control Number: 2025915793

Table of Contents

Dedication 1

Introduction 3

Dogs 5

Food 21

Depression Expression 29

Spiritual Musings 51

Social Consciousness 74

Sonnets 84

Limericks 89

A Little of This. A Little of That. 94

Poems I Didn't Write 117

Alphabetical Index of Poems 125

Acknowledgements 130

Previous Books by Christina J Donato 131

About the Author 132

Social Media 133

Dedication

This book is dedicated to all who inspired these poems over the course of my lifetime. Whether good, bad, or indifferent, I couldn't have written this book without you.

Introduction

You picked up my book. Did the title catch your eye, or the cover? The book cover was created using Microsoft Designer.

An *olio* is a miscellaneous collection, a hodgepodge of seemingly unrelated works.
In this book you will find poems of many lengths, styles and subjects. Some are funny. Some are serious. Some are light. Some are dark, very dark.

There are nine sections. Each one ends with background information about the individual poems. If you just read these without reading the poems you would learn a lot about the author. If you read the poems without reading the background information, you may learn something about yourself.

I consider poetry to be a literary medium for the eyes and ears, as well as the mind of the reader. Look at the shapes of the stanza outlines.

Look at the words themselves. Are they complicated or simple? Are they nonsensical? Do they contain eye rhymes, such as the words *laughter* and *daughter*.

After absorbing the poems with your eyes, read them out loud, or have them read to you. What is their cadence? Is it awkward, does it flow like a sweet melody, or does it have the tempo of a march? Consider the sound of the words rather than just their meaning.

Dogs

I Won't Go Straight to Heaven

I won't go straight to heaven
on the day that I do die.

I'll stop first, along the way,
at the rainbow bridge on high.
Where all the dogs I have loved
will all gather at my feet.

We'll continue toward heaven
where life will be oh so sweet.

Terri Featherhead

We met in a department store
when I was seven.
I'd always go to see the pets
when my parents went shopping.

You were only eight weeks old,
small, wiggly, yapping.
Mom and Dom were with me that day.
If I could get Dom on my side, just maybe...

My big brother, who was all of nine,
chimed in with me: "Can we have her?
Can we take her home?!"
Mom said we'd have to ask Dad.

Terri, I never wanted to see Dad so much
as that day you and I met.
Dad made us look at some other dogs,
But our young minds were firmly set.

Back to Dad who took out his wallet.
He pulled out fifty dollars.
Wow! We must be rich.
After all, it was 1966.

Off to the store we all went,
Mom, Dad, Dom, and I.
"Are you sure you want this little thing?"
"Yes. Yes! We already have a name."

Now you were ours, a Toy Fox Terrier
with a white feather shape on your head.
"Terri Featherhead," we shouted.
And Terri Featherhead you became.

You were with us almost 16 years.
The day you left, we were all in tears.
Even Dad grew to love our little 7-pound dog
With a big personality, and lots of love.

The week after you died was the longest week.
A dogless house is not a home.
So I adopted Belle. She's another story.
I went to your grave to ask you to forgive me.

Please forgive me, Terri. You cannot be replaced
But I missed coming home to a furry face.
Then and forever, I love. I love you.

Ding Dong Belle

On a trip to NSAL*
My mom and I met little Belle.
Six weeks old, with black and white fur,
We asked a man if we could hold her.

He placed her on a mantle.
She was quiet, not making a peep,
'cause a lot she had been handled,
And just wanted to get some sleep.

Along came two young men
To check out a cute little kitten
From their looks my mom and I
could tell they were smitten.

But the kitten caught Belle's eye,
And in a flash, she dashed to its side.
My mom grabbed Belle just in time.
And I decided she had to be mine.

Belle was taken to the back
so the staff could fill her gift packet.
When suddenly Mom and I heard
A dog screaming and making a racket.

From the back of the place
We heard someone say
They felt sorry for the people
adopting her that day.

Mom and I looked at each other.
I shook my head as I said to my mother
"I think we're in for trouble with this one,
My mom chimed in, "Oh brother!"

When we got her back home,
We all hugged and kissed her.
We decided she'd be Belle,
The name of Snoopy's sister.

That first night Belle cried,
Nothing would appease her.
She never stopped whining,
Nothing seemed to please her.

Her cuteness was abundant.
She never did anyone harm.
She even learned to say some words
Such as "I love you, Mom."

I know that is hard to believe,
Yet other people heard it.
It was years before cell phones so
You'll have to take my word for it.

She didn't like playing games,
But she liked seeing the doc.
Throughout her entire life
She just had one toy sock.

Belle loved eating apples,
And snuggling close as well.
I loved her so much,
My beating heart would swell.

*North Shore Animal League

Never Believe a Puppy

Never believe a puppy
that wants to come home with you.
Never believe a puppy.
They'll never tell the truth.

They'll act so cute, and lick your face,
and wiggle at your feet.
But take them home, they cry and moan, until you
scream – I'M BEAT!

Their antics never end,
not even through the night.
And when you try to comfort or scold,
all they do is bite!

So, never believe a puppy
that wants to come home with you.
Never believe a puppy.
They'll never tell the truth.

Maybe they acted frisky.
Maybe they acted meek.
They seem to know just what to do
to make the strongest weak.

You thought they had the cutest ears,
whether up or down.
Now when you try to sneak a snack,
those ears hear every sound!

Oh, never believe a puppy
that wants to come home with you.
Never believe a puppy.
I'm telling you; they'll never tell the truth.

Their big brown eyes said ,
"Love me, please."
Their tail just wagged away.
You never suspect it's all a tease,
until they're home to stay.

They chew your things, dig up your trees,
and eat just like a HOG.
The only thing that keeps you sane,
is to know they will soon be a DOG!

The Freckles Song

I'm a boy. I'm a boy.
I bring my mother so much joy.

I'm a boy. I'm a boy.
I'm more fun than your favorite toy.

I'm a male. I'm a male.
I bring smiles. I never fail.

I'm a male. I'm a male.
See me wag my furry tail.

I'm a boy. I'm a boy.
I bring all my friends lots of joy.

I'm a boy. I'm a boy.
I'm more fun than your favorite toy.

A Walking Day

It's a walking day.
We're gonna sniff everything along the way.
There's a tree. There's a pole.
There's a bush. There's a hole!
There's some poop. There's a rock.
Look over there – it's someone's sock!

It's a walking day.
We're gonna sniff everything along the way.
There's a bag. There's a hat.
Don't hold me back – I see a cat!
There's a leaf. There's a toy.
Let's go sniff - that little boy!

It's a walking day.
We're gonna sniff everything along the way.
There's a branch. There's a nut.
There's a dog. Let's sniff her butt!
There's a coin. There's a notch.
There's a man. Let's sniff his crotch!

It's a walking day. Let's sniff!

Section Poem Backgrounds

I Won't Go Straight to Heaven
I don't even remember writing this one.

Terri Featherhead
Our first family dog. The poem says it all.

Ding Dong Belle
Belle was my second dog. We adopted her from the North Shore Animal League (NSAL). She inspired my illustrated children's chapter book *The Saddest Dog Finds a Friend.*

Never Believe a Puppy
It's all about Bibi, a black & white pointer mix. Just a few weeks old when I adopted her, she was a handful. I nicknamed her The Noun Buster because she destroyed people, places, and things. When she grew up, she was delightfully obedient.

Being outside was her happy place. As much as she was outside, she naturally learned and preferred to do her business there. She was the easiest dog to housetrain.

Until her final days, Bibi never had an accident in the house. Never.

The Freckles Song

Freckles was my heart dog. I always wanted a purebred beagle. When I heard there was a place nearby with beagles to adopt, I headed straight there. They had a male and a female. I never intended to adopt a male. However, the female would not approach me. The male did. I picked him up and saw that his nose was sprinkled with light brown freckles. I told him, "A good name for you would be Freckles." At that point I figured that since I named him, he was mine.

It's a Walking Day

My sweet Grady. Like any respectful hound dog, he was a sniffer. Two steps and
stop. Another two steps and stop. One day I decided I would not prod him along. We would stop when he stopped and walk when he walked. A walk that usually took about 20 minutes took almost an hour and a half! He is featured in my children's chapter book *The Dog Who Wanted to be Human.*

Food

Ice Cream

"I scream. You Scream. We all
Scream for ice cream." You know
those words, I'm sure. We all yelled them
at an ice cream truck, and when in the ice
cream store. People of all ages - young,
middle-aged, and old, have a favorite flavor,
if the truth be told. Now here's the top ten
list from *USA Today*, it was published in
July of ' 24. Here's what it had to say:
Peanut butter cup comes in at number
ten. Rocky Road is number nine.
Chocolate Chip is eight. Mint
Chocolate Chip is seven. The
list is mighty fine. Cookies
and Cream is number six,
but I'd rate it even
higher. Landing at
number five is
Cookie Dough.
The list is now
on fire. Number

four is Butter
Pecan, and
number three
is Strawberry.
Wondering
what the top
two are – or
are you get-
ting weary?
Since the
runner up
is choco-
late, I'm
sure that
you can
guess,
good
old
smooth Vanilla is rated as the best. Your
favorite flavor, that at will make you
wait in line a while, may differ from
mine, my friend, but it's sure to make
you smile. I cannot cry when eating ice

cream. I don't feel sad and blue. I always
smile while it is in my mouth. And that's
the truest truth.

Ode to Cheddar Cheese

Cheese Cheddar cheese,
Oh, Cheddar cheese.
There's nothing like it I have ever tasted.
When I eat it nothing's ever wasted.

Cheddar cheese, Oh, Cheddar cheese.
So, if it's me that a man would like to please,
He better have a lot of Cheddar cheese.

Cake without Frosting is a Muffin

I love cake:
Fluffy, firm, moist, or flakey.
I won't give it up,
No, you cannot make me.

I love frosting:
Thick, buttery, creamy, and vanilla.
If a man is a baker, He's my kind of fella.

Chocolate, mocha Strawberry or cream cheese will do.
The thicker the better, I say to you.

I won't eat cake that hasn't been frosted.
But I will eat frosting that hasn't been caked.

Section Poem Backgrounds

Ice Cream

This is a concrete poem about one of my favorite foods. I will bow to the online Merriam-Webster Dictionary to define concrete poetry.

":poetry in which the poet's intent is conveyed by the graphic patterns of letters, words, or symbols rather than by the conventional arrangement of words."

This is not my first attempt to write a concrete poem. I did one in high school. This is my latest, written in January of 2025. Not only is its topic one of my favorite foods, but it is also shaped like a single scoop ice cream cone standing upright on a dish.

Ode to Cheddar Cheese

I wrote this tribute to Cheddar in my late twenties.

Cake without Frosting is a Muffin

Another favorite food.

Depression Expression

***WARNING** – Some of the poems in the section are raw and deeply dark. This may make them difficult to read for some.*

Another Day

Another day is over, I say.
No one cared I was alive today.

And if tomorrow I deem to be
The day that I die,
No one would even notice,
Nor wonder why.

At Last

At last! I have shed my mortal shell.
Done now are the trials that life did befell.
Please don't give me nary another thought,
for gone is the anguish that life had wrought.

I put in my time. I was steadfast and true.
I'm no longer scared, tired, alone, or blue.
The darkness of life, I leave it behind.
I'm now out of my body, instead of out of my mind.

I'm living in Joy and surrounded by Love.
I'm embracing the glory of heaven above.
Reunited with loved ones both people and pets.
Where I am now is as good as it gets.

Epitaph # 1

I'm no longer lonely.
I'm no longer sad.
Oh, what a blessing
It is to be dead.

Except Jesus

Nobody loves me.
Nobody cares, except Jesus.
Nobody's hoping that
I would be theirs, except Jesus.

I've felt alone all of my years.
I don't even have a home.
I wash my pillow in my own tears.
Nobody even phones.

But Jesus, He loves me.
Jesus, He wants me.
His word, it tells me so.

He won't deceive me.
He'll never leave me,
not even when I'm feeling low.

Oh, nobody loves me.
Nobody cares, except Jesus.

I have no friends and no family
So I roam from town to town.

I tell people I meet
that I don't accept defeat,
'cause Jesus is always around.

Yes, Jesus, He loves me.
Jesus, He wants me.
His word, it tells me so.

He won't deceive me.
He'll never leave me,
not even when I'm feeling low.

And when nobody loves you,
and nobody cares
except Jesus – you're doing alright.

I Ask You

Where do the unwanted people go?
Where do the unloved end up?
Where do the loneliest people go,
When they have had enough?

Is there a place where there's no loneliness?
Is there a place where there is no pain?
Where do the unwanted people go,
I ask you once again?

Some people are like dogs in a kennel,
Too old for someone to want.
They're wounded and scarred –
Not healthy by far.
Unadoptable, that's what some people are.

Some people are like abandoned buildings,
Slated for the wrecking ball.
They are a sore sight.
They cause children fright.
And are ignored by one and by all.

Some people are like wilted flowers,
Left in the hot sun too long.
Dried out and burned, never to learn
Where the refreshing waters come from.

Where do the uncared for people go?
Where do the forgotten end up?
Where do the ones there's no time for go,
When they have had enough?

Is there a place where there's no loneliness?
Is there a place where there is no pain?
Where do the uncared for people go,
I ask you once again?

And what do we do until then?

I'm Living Because I was Born

I'm living because I was born.
I don't have any friends,
Except the friends that I've got.

If this poem sounds a little forlorn,
It's 'cause I'm only living,
Yes, I'm only living,
I'm living because I was born.

I'm living because I was born.
Don't have much going for me,
No love of my own.
And because of my acts
My freedom is blown.

So if this poem sounds a little forlorn,
That's 'cause I'm only living,
Yes, I'm only living,
I'm living because I was born.

I'm living because I was born.
One day I'll be paroled
And move on from this place.
The dark side of life,
A fall from His grace.

If this poem sounds a little forlorn,
It's 'cause I'm only living,
Yes, I'm only living,
I'm living because I was born.

Life is a Gift?

I've heard it said that life is a gift.
What do you do if it just doesn't fit?
It's rude to return it, and hard to re-gift.
It's a waste to not use it, at least a little bit.

So I'll listen to music, and play with my dog,
Relish the sunshine and hide from the fog.
Sometimes I'll stroll, and sometimes I'll jog.
And once in a while , I'll just sit on a log.

I'll partake of food from all over the world,
Buy a diamond or two and maybe a pearl,
Delight in a butterfly, see my dog chase a squirrel.
I could open a brothel, but I'm not that kind of girl.

I could rent some old movies, watch too much T.V.
Meet a friend for some coffee or for a spot of tea,
Hang out with my boyfriend, if I knew who he'd be.
Maybe it's my beagle. I know he loves me.

I like to visit zoos
and travel all around.
I've been to Europe four times,
returning home safe and sound.

I've been to the circus,
but I don't laugh at any clown.
I enjoyed the World's Fair in '66,
and wish it was still around.

I'd like to go overseas again,
because I've yet to get to France.
I'd go to sip champagne and wine
and give the Eiffel Tower a glance.

Just thinking of the cheese and pastries
sets my heart to dance.
I'd probably gain 20 pounds,
but I think it's worth the chance.

I don't like gardening,
but I love all kinds of flowers.
I can admire mountain scenery
for hours and for hours.

I know that God loves me;
it's part of His unearthly powers.
His creation is for all of us –
in other words, it's ours.

I mourn for what's been lost –
my parents and my youth.
I try not to lie,
but it's hard to face the truth.

My loneliness hurts,
like the cut of a tooth.
I guess I could swear,
but I know that's uncouth.

Or So I Thought

Secrets revealed that made me hideous,
the evil within me expressed.
Subhuman traits both physical and mental,
were the causes of my duress.

Nobody could care for me,
or so I thought.
Nobody could love me,
or so I thought.
Nobody could want me,
or so I thought.

The Way That He Tells Me

My man says he loves me.
I don't see how he can.
No one else has ever loved me.
Not any other man.
Yet, the way that he tells me,
I believe him.

My man says I'm pretty.
I know this can't be true.
When I look into the mirror,
I can see the cold hard truth.
Yet, the way that he tells me,
I believe him.

My man says I'm sweet and smart.
"Rather bittersweet," I reply.
He must be seeing me with his heart.
For I'm truly sour deep inside.
Yet, the way that he tells me,
I believe him.

My man says I'm lovely,
Even when I'm sad.
But I know that I'm ugly,
Even when I'm glad.
Yet, the way that he tells me,
I believe him.

There's a Fool in this World

There's a fool, in this world,
who is waiting to be fooled,
into thinking he can fall in love with me,
and he'll fall in love with me.
There's a fool in this world.

If you see me walking down
the street with a man,
please don't tell him who I am.
Sooner or later he's bound to see,
just how unlovable and
undesirable I can be.
Sooner or later he's bound to see,
he was a fool to fall in love with me.

But, there's a fool, in this world,
who is waiting to be fooled,
into thinking he can fall in love with me,
and he'll fall in love with me.
Where can he be?

I wrote those words as a teenager.
Now I am older and wiser.
I've learned to live without love.
It's a hard way.
That I'm still waiting for the fool to appear,
I can no longer say.

If not for God and my dogs,
I'd never have known affection.
Never in my lonely life have I
held a man's attention.

Poor Little Girl

Poor little girl. Poor little girl.

Nobody loves me.
No, no one ever could.
It's a human impossibility.

Poor little girl. Poor little girl.

Section Poem Backgrounds

Another Day

I have experienced bouts of major depression as far back as I can remember. Depression has been a great inspiration for composing poetry.
This poem is one of the saddest I have written. I wrote it when I was fifteen years old.

At Last

I wrote this upon returning from a funeral. The funeral prompted me to think about what I would want written on the funeral cards at my wake. This poem is what I created.

The last stanza was added much later, on a better day.

Not your typical funeral card.

Epitaph # 1

Short and bitter.

Except Jesus
Like many of my poems, this one started out as a song. It could have been put in the Spiritual Musings section. However, I wrote it when I was in a major depression, so I placed it here.

I Ask You
Another depression inspired poem.

I'm Living Because I was Born
This started as a song. I imagined someone sitting in a jail cell, strumming an old guitar, and singing with a southern twang.

Life is a Gift?
This one is much lighter in tone than the previous ones. I was trying to think positive thoughts in my despair. At this point my Christian faith was growing deeper, influencing my choice of words.

Or So I Thought
Another poem influenced by my faith. I wrote the first stanza in my typical fashion. Then, I tried to

counteract my feelings of hopelessness with what I was learning about God.

The Way that He Tells Me
This one was written in 2025. My husband and I have been together for 18 years. Will I ever see myself the way he sees me?

There's a Fool in this World
Back to the beginning with another poem I wrote when I was fifteen. Thirty years later I wrote the second half of the poem. It took another two years before I met said fool. We married when I was 64 and he was 71. It is the first marriage for both of us.

Poor Little Girl
This is yet another poem written on yet another sad and lonely day.

Spiritual Musings

Dear Abba

I thought I'd take the time to write,
To thank you for the gifts you gave me.
The sun and moon and stars and life,
And all the other gifts you gave me.

For all my friends and family.
But most of all for your Son, Jesus.
His life for mine is the greatest gift.
One you don't ask me to repay,
(As if I could do it anyway).

One day I'll meet you face to face.
At the big family reunion.
We'll be together ever more –
All of us, your children.

For all these many gifts and more,
Too many to ever mention.
I know that you're not keeping score.
Thank you for your attention.

He is One of a Kind

He came down to earth.
It was a virgin birth.
That Jesus, He is one of a kind.

He grew up and got baptized.
Then he started preaching.
That Jesus, He is one of a kind.

He fasted forty days,
Resisted the devil.
That Jesus, He is one of a kind.

He chose himself some apostles.
Gathered some disciples.
That Jesus, He is one of a kind.

He preached to all the Good News.
He did many kinds of miracles.
That Jesus, He is one of a kind.

He cast out some demons.
He told a bunch of parables.
That Jesus, He is one of a kind.

Betrayed by Judas.
Died upon a cross.
That Jesus, He is one of a kind.

He rose up on the third day.
Then He ascended to heaven.
That Jesus, He is one of a kind.

He's at the Father's side,
'Til he returns again.
That Jesus, He is one of a kind.

We'll all rise up to meet him.
Angels will help us greet him.
That Jesus, He is one of a kind.

That Jesus, He is one.
That Jesus is the One.
That Jesus, He is one of a kind.

Jesus is a Loving Savior

Jesus is a loving Savior.
He helps me through my woes,
Protects me from my foes,
Forgives me my indiscretions
Of things only heaven knows.

Jesus is the perfect Savior.
He shows me perfect ways,
To make it through my days.
He sets the perfect example
Of what I should do and say.

Jesus is a living Savior.
He died on the cross for me,
Then He rose again, you see.
So now I have His promise
Of life eternally.

Jesus is the only Savior.
He sits at the Father's side,
Oversees things far and wide.
His blood, it purifies me
So, one day I'll be his bride.

Let's Shout His Name

God is wonderful. Let's shout His name!
God is beautiful. Let's shout His name!

Jehovah. Yahweh. Father. I Am.
Elohim. Abba. Strong-hold. The One.

God is wonderful. Let's shout His name!
God is beautiful. Let's shout His name!

Messiah. Savior. Rabbi. The Word.
Good Shepherd. Bridegroom. First Born.
The Lord.

God is wonderful. Let's shout His name!
God is beautiful. Let's shout His name!

Comforter. Guider. Helper. God's Breath.
Good Spirit. Witness. Teacher of truth.

God is wonderful. Let's shout His name!
God is beautiful. Let's shout His name!

The Lord Sends Rain

The Lord sends rain, and it is fine.
Now there is fruit on the vine.

Alleluia, alleluia
The Lord sends rain, and it is fine.

The Lord sends sunshine, hour after hour.
Now on the plant, there is a flower.

Alleluia, alleluia
The Lord sends sunshine, hour after hour.

The Lord sends love, for you and me.
Now we are like a family.

Alleluia, alleluia
The Lord sends love, for you and me.

The Lord sent the, preacher so he can teach.
Now we know ,the depths of God's reach.

Alleluia, alleluia
The Lord sent the preacher, so he can teach.

The Lord allows troubles, sometimes to the brim.
Now we know, we can count on Him.

Alleluia, alleluia
The Lord allows troubles, sometimes to the brim.

The Lord, He forgives me, no matter what I do.
So now I learn, how to forgive you.

Alleluia, alleluia
The Lord he forgives, me no matter what I do.

The Lord came to earth, to suffer great strife.
Now we have eternal life.

Alleluia, alleluia
The Lord came to earth, to suffer great strife.

The Lord will come again, so we can be together.
No more will there be, stormy weather.

Alleluia, alleluia
The Lord will come again, so we can be together.

The Lord sends rain.
The Lord sends sunshine.
The Lord sends love.
The Lord sends the preacher.

The Lord allows troubles.
The Lord does forgive me.
The Lord came to earth.
The Lord will come again.

We Raise One Voice to You

Powerful, merciful,
Knowing, giving –
Such is the Father God.

Unchanging, omniscient,
Present, Sovereign –
Such is the Father God.

We praise and worship You.
We raise one voice to You.
The Father, and the Son,
And the Holy Spirit, too.

Glorious victory,
Teaching, loving –
Such is the Lamb of God.

Forgiving, compassionate,
Servant, prayerful –
Such is the Lamb of God.

We praise and worship You.
We raise one voice to You.
The Father, and the Son,
And the Holy Spirit, too.

Comforting, joyful,
Cleansing, willing –
Such is the Spirit of God.

Indwelling, empowering,
Fruit bearing, mindful –
Such is the Spirit of God.

We praise and worship You.
We raise one voice to You.
The Father, and the Son,
And the Holy Spirit, too.

Imitators of Jesus

We are imitators of Jesus.
We aim to be like Him all day.
We are imitators of Jesus.
We will always follow His way.

Become imitators of Jesus,
Like those who are walking Christ's way.
Unlike enemies of Lord Jesus.
We weep as we tell you they strayed.

Their gods are their very own bellies,
Rejoicing in their acts of shame.
Evil focused on their world of sin.
Refusing to honor God's name.

As we're imitators of Jesus,
We are citizens upon High,
From whence our remarkable Jesus
Returns as His rapture draws nigh.

He will transform all of our bodies,
To conform to His glorious one;
With His power to subdue all things,
As He is the Father God's son.

We are imitators of Jesus.
We aim to be like Him all day.
We are imitators of Jesus.
We will always follow His way.

Jesus' Love

With so much to lose,
I'm a hundredfold blessed.
I have so much more
than so many of the rest.

Take away my health.
Make me sick every day.
Cover me with boils.
Take my sight away.

Make my cupboard empty.
Take my food away.
Take away my water.
Set my thirst to stay.

Take away my family.
Take away my friends.
Lock me in a dungeon,
until my life does end.

Take away my money.
Make my savings go.
Take away my job.
Leave me nothing left to show.

Whether I am sick, or hungry,
or lonely or poor,
With Jesus' love I need no more.

My Wish

If I could wish a wish, the wish I'd wish is this:

> That the lonely would feel loved,
> Because they are loved by God.
>
> That the discarded would feel wanted,
> Because they are wanted by God.
>
> That the lowly would feel important,
> Because they are important to God.

God Says

God says I'm wonderful.
Who am I to disagree?
When our opinions differ
It is not Him that's wrong - it's me.

God says I'm unique.
That is good to know.
Earth couldn't handle another
Of what to this world I show.

God says I'm special.
He's created me for a task.
He will give me what I need.
So all I must do is ask.

God says I'm lovely.
Created to shine so bright.
With His word to guide me
The stars will bow down to my light.

God says I'm precious.
He sent His Son to pay the price.
If only I believe in Him ,
Christ's sacrifice will full suffice.

God says I'm strong.
I can beat the vilest foe.
His truth keeps me safe.
I can defeat the devil's blow.

God says I'm chosen.
He picked me for His own.
Spiritually adopted.
Flesh of His flesh, bone of His bone.

All this that God says I am
He says about you, too.
Just believe Christ is your savior
And you'll make this poem about you.

Section Poem Backgrounds

Jesus is a Loving Savoir

I was prolific in 2001, writing several Praise and Worship songs, including this one. I had the collection copyrighted under the name of C-Notes (C for Christina, Christian, and the key in which the songs were in).

Dear Abba

I wrote this one in the early 2000s. A few years later the lyrics were printed in the weekly bulletin of the church I was attending at that time. A friend of mine liked it so much, she made a copy to keep in her Bible. She told me she reads it regularly.

He is One of a Kind

Written in 2001 as a Praise and Worship song, it was performed as special music with someone else singing.

Let's Shout His Name

The songs in C-Notes seemed to come out of

nowhere. This one was no exception. God blessed me with a way with words, and a love of music. Unfortunately for any listeners, He decided I didn't need a good voice to sing them.

The Lord Sends Rain

This is one of my favorite Praise and Worship songs from C- Notes. The lines are simple, as in a nursery rhyme. When I was asked by a Sunday school teacher if this song/poem could be used to teach his children in Bible school, I happily gave my permission.

We Raise One Voice to You

From C-Notes, this poem spotlights the many names and functions of the Holy Trinity.

Imitators of Jesus

My newest poem/song. It came to mind while listening to a sermon on Philippians 3:17-21, ESV Translation. I liked the flow of the words, so I started singing it in my head.

"Brothers, join in imitating me, and keep your eyes on

those who walk according to the example you have in us.

For many, of whom I have often told you and now tell you even with tears, walk as enemies of the cross of Christ.

Their end is destruction, their god is their belly, and they glory in their shame, with minds set on   earthly things.

But our citizenship is in heaven, and from it we await a Savior, the Lord Jesus Christ, who will transform our lowly body to be like his glorious body, by the power that enables him even to subject all things to himself."

Jesus' Love

A poem inspired by the faithful in the Bible who, even in the toughest times, put their relationship with the Lord above all else. To name a few: Job, John the Baptist, and the Apostle Paul.

My Wish

A short poem, and to the point. This could

have been placed in the Depression Expression chapter. I was the lonely, discarded, and lowly person I wanted to encourage.

God Says

This poem, from February 2025, was inspired by my kitchen floor mats. I'm not fully convinced that the Bible verses used to illustrate each item on the mats completely describe the traits, but I do believe the traits printed on the mats are true.

Social Consciousness

I Painted Myself

I painted myself black just the other day,
To see what my father would say.
"Negro, Negro, get out of my house!"
"But Dad, it's me."
"Negro, Negro, get out of my house!"
"But Dad, it's I."
"Negro, Negro get out of my house!"

I left.

I painted myself yellow just the other day,
To see what my father would say.
"Chink, Chink, get out of my house!"
"But Dad, it's me."
"Chink, Chink, get out of my house!"
"But Dad, it's I."
"Chink, Chink, get out of my house!"

I left.

I painted myself brown just the other day,
To see what my father would say.
"Spic, Spic, get out of my house!"
"But Dad, it's me."
"Spic, Spic, get out of my house!"
"But Dad, it's I."
"Spic, Spic, get out of my house!"

I left.

I painted myself red just the other day,
To see what my father would say.
"Injun, Injun, get out of my house!"
"But Dad, it's me."
"Injun, Injun, get out of my house!"
"But Dad, it's I."
"Injun, Injun, get out of my house!"

I left.

I painted myself white just the other day, To see
what my father would say.
"Honky, Honky, get out of my house!" "But Dad,
it's me."
"Honky, Honky, get out of my house!" "But Dad,
it's I."
"Honky, Honky, get out of my house!"

I left.

I washed off the paint just the other day, To see
what my father would say.
"Daughter, Daughter, where have you been?"

I Want to be a Member of the Rich

I want to be a member of the rich,
in a classless society.
I want to be a member of the elite.
I'll even settle for the bourgeoisie.

I want to be the one with all the power
to tell everyone else what to do,
and how to do it, and how to think it,
and how to act, and what to feel.
I want to do all this in a place
that never exploits any member
of the human race.

I want to be a member of the great,
where the dream of a good life has not faded,
where there's work for everyone,
and no one ever feels alienated.

I want to be a member of the best,
in the world's greatest nation,
where you can be whatever you want
after your state planned education.

Where is this place I dream of?
Where is this place I long to be?
Is it near? Is it far?
Is it here or the U.S.S.R?

When I Look into the Face
Part One

When I look into the face of my spouse to be
I see these things that could never be me:

The rich color of fertile soil.
The spicy brown of a cinnamon stick.
The golden shade of an autumn leaf.
The tall, broad strength of redwood.
The sweet color of a Muscatel grape.

These are like the colors of autumn leaves
Floating in the midday sky.

All these hues are shades of brown
And in me they could never be found,
For I am white.

When I Look into the Face
Part Two

When I look into the face of my spouse to be
I see these things that could never be me:

Fair pink rose petals.
The blush of champagne.
The color of buttercream.
Sunshine yellow.
And a field of blue cornflowers.

All these things are bright and fresh
As a perfectly ripe peach
Resting in newly fallen snow.

All these things are shades of white
In me they are found very slight
For I am black.

Section Poem Backgrounds

I Painted Myself

This poem is from high school, when I was becoming aware of social issues. It's easy to skim through, and it does have a point. I'll leave it to you to figure it out.

I wrestled with whether I should use the original wording. Some words are offensive to many. I could have changed them to make them politically correct, but I feel that waters down the ending's impact.

I Want to be a Member of the Rich

I majored in Political Science and Sociology in college. This poem was included at the end of a paper I wrote on communism. Bear in mind, it was the 1980s when the USSR still existed, was powerful, and was our number one enemy.

Empire State College called the professors *mentors*. My mentor paid me high praise when he told me the poem sounded like something John Lennon would have written.

Things in My Love That in Me Could Never Be Found

At the time I wrote this, I had a white woman friend with a porcelain complexion whose boyfriend was a dark-skinned black man.

Sonnets

Loving Luv – A Shakespearean Sonnet

Loving love with Luv each day is lovely.
Being in love with Luv is so sublime.
Daytime starts off so great when Luv hugs me.
Loving with Luv each night I feel so fine.

I am loved with Luv's entire being.
It's divine each time we come together.
Luv's love will always keep me from fleeing.
Our love keeps our hearts light as a feather.

Missing Luv's love each morn when Luv leaves me,
Even knowing Luv will love me each night,
Hours pass slowly and it bereaves me,
Dawn and dusk together would make it right.

I love Luv with all my heart and my soul.
Each a half, together we make a whole.

Loving Luv – A Petrarchan Sonnet

Loving love with Luv each day is lovely.
Being in love with Luv is so sublime.
Loving with Luv each night I feel so fine.
Daytime starts off so great when Luv hugs me.

I am loved with Luv's entire being.
It's divine each time we come together.
Our love keeps our hearts light as a feather.
Luvs's love will always keep me from fleeing.

Missing Luv's love each morn when Luv leaves me,
Even knowing Luv will love me each night.
Putting dawn and dusk close would make me smile.
Nay the hours apart they bereave me.
My love with Luv makes my heart new and bright.
Hearts forever together all the while.

Section Poem Backgrounds

Loving Luv – A Shakespearean sonnet

I well as I can remember, this is my first attempt at writing a sonnet. Depending on where you research, there are four to eight types of sonnets.

This one is written in the Shakespearean or English format. The rhyme scheme is ABAB CDCD EFEF GG.

I purposely do not use any pronouns so that the reader can imagine who the sonnet is written about.

Loving Luv - Petrarchan sonnet

The rhyming scheme for this type of sonnet is ABBA ABBA CDCCDC or ABBA ABBA CDECDE. I chose the latter scheme for my sonnet.

Here I take the Shakespearean sonnet and convert it to a Petrarchan or Italian one. That is not as easy as it may sound.

I'm used to rhyming two consecutive lines or every other line. This format requires two lines in between the rhyming one for some of the lines. It is a foreign pattern to my eyes and ears.

It was not easy for me to come up with so many lines about love whereas writing about despair or the absence of love just flows from me.

The past two years have been the happiest ones in my life. However, painful memories run deep, often too deep to erase.

Limericks

Limerick #1

There was a fair maiden from Cranston,
Who lived in a beautiful mansion.
Things got so weird,
When her chin grew a beard.
Now she's not pretty, she's handsome.

Limerick #2

There once was a boy with a bucket
He'd swing it and then he would chuck it.
It hit a girl's head,
And soon she was dead.
If only she learned how to duck it.

Limerick #3

I once knew a dog named Nera.
Who stared at herself in a mirror.
One day the glass broke,
Giving Nera a stroke.
Now mirrors dear Nera has fear of.

Limerick #4

There once was a fellow named Ernie
Who was a criminal attorney.
He'd lose without fail
Landing his clients in jail
'Til he was found in the morgue on a gurney.

Limerick #5

Boomers are still the best rockers.
They keep all their pot in their lockers.
It's now legal you see,
But it sure isn't free.
So they keep it away from the stalkers.

Limerick # 6

There once was a man named McGuire
Who was the town drunk and a liar.
When he drank up his beer,
He no longer had fear.
So he laughed while his pants were on fire.

Section Poem Backgrounds

Limericks #1 - #6

Editing this book got me thinking about other types of poetry I might want to include here. Limericks came to mind. I hope you enjoy them as much as I did writing them.

A Little of This. A Little of That.

The Golden Years

Two young lovers strolling side by side,
That was you and I so long ago.
Holding each other's hands, beaming with pride.
The years gone by; how swiftly they flow!

In our middle years we held on tight,
Raising children, making a house a home.
Our hearts were full though money was slight.
We cried when our children decided to roam.

And now what are called our Golden Years,
They are reaching so near to our door.
We are now finally rid of our fears,
Of what all our future years have in store.

And so our days are short,
Our lives almost done.
In heaven when we pick our roommates,
you will be the one.

I am...

I am...
awed by abilities,
bruised by bashing,
cut by criticism,
delighted by dreams,
excited by enthusiasm,
fueled by food,
graced by God,
humbled by humility,
incensed by ignorance,
jubilant by joy,
kayoed by kindness,
lured by love,
mired by madness,
nurtured by niceness,
outraged by outrage,
pleased by positivity,
quelled by quirkiness,
restored by righteousness,

spellbound by serenity,
tickled by triumph,
uplifted by understanding,
vitalized by victory,
wowed by wisdom,
xeroxed by x-rays,
yielded by youth,
zonked by zeal.

Another Birthday

Many years ago (in the 1900's) I was snug, safe, and warm. I was comforted by my mom's heartbeat and the occasional eclectic tunes of her digestive juices.

Then, without warning, some man (a doctor) took a knife (scalpel) and plunged it into my mother's abdomen and into her uterus. I was yanked out into this noisy, bright, cold, and scary world against my will - six weeks early.

I've always felt the cosmos owes me those six weeks of secure serenity where all my needs were being met. I never got them back. Sure, sure, a few hours here and a few days there, but never those six weeks of uninterrupted solitude.

None of us asks to be born. In fact, my Facebook motto Is "I'm living because I was born." Aren't we all? Today I acknowledge the completion of another orbit around the sun and the beginning of another one. I don't know if I will complete this one or if I will have those six weeks within it.

I'm sure it will be a year of ups and downs, looking into the future and remembering the past, new adventures, anxieties, pleasures, health, sickness, hesitant hopes, and expected tears.

Well, here goes...

The Loss of a Loved One

The loss of a loved one can be painful indeed. You
feel helpless and hopeless and greatly in need.
Time heals all wounds, that is what people say.
It's hard to believe, no matter how much you pray.

Find comfort in memories of times together.
Love is a glue that holds on forever.
There will be things to look forward to again.
Although this is true, I can't tell you when.

Know that you're thought of, cared for and loved,
The next time you gaze at the stars up above.
There will be one more star shining so brightly,
As your loved one watches over you nightly.

On Your Wedding Day

May your marriage be like the moon –
Something to depend on,
Romantic,
Rarely blue,
Often full,
A light amidst darkness,
And Heavenly made.

Christmas Ditties

One:
At this time of Christmas cheer,
So very close to a brand new year,
This wish is sent for all the best:
Good food and drink with your holiday fest.

Two:
When wrapping up your Christmas presents,
Think of all the poor little peasants,
Who don't celebrate the Christmas Day.
But at least they won't have bills to pay.

Three:
For all of you, here are six wishes:
Health. Wealth. Love. Smiles. Fun.
And a maid to do the dirty dishes.

Four:
At this time of year when people can
be so phony...
... at least you can count on
your alimony.

Five:
Ho, ho, ho's,
Mistletoe,
Candy canes,
And lots of snow.

Six:
holly... mistletoe... nativity... reindeer...
candy canes... presents... evergreens...
pinecones... Santa... nutcrackers...
Christmas words all strung in a line,
bringing greetings to you and yours,
from me and mine.

Seven:
Ho. Ho. Ho.
Hee. Hee. Hee.
What kind of present did you get for me?

My Dad

Sometimes he treats me.
Sometimes he beats me.
But he's mine all mine

Fancy Pantsy

Fancy pantsy is what they said,
Wishy washy in garlic bread.
From the toilet to the pipe,
Boy what a terrible sight!

Roses are Red

Rose are red.
Violets are blue.
La da da de da.
La da da de do.

I Went Down a Falls

I went down a falls.
Niagara in a barrel.
Nails pierced through my sides.
I paid ten cents for this ride.
I want my dime back.

A Mom's Birthday

This is for the mom who
made me take cooking lessons, who made me take
sewing lessons, who made me clean my room.
who made me apologize to my brother...

Who made me.

Happy birthday, from one of the best things you
ever made
(Since you are such a wonderful mother, I know
you will agree)
I'm proud to be the apple that has fallen not far
from the tree.

A Dad's Birthday

This is for the dad who
made me take swimming lessons,
who made me take music lessons,
who made me take the training wheels off my bicycle...

Who made me.

Happy birthday, from one of the best things you ever
made
(Since you are such a wonderful father, I know you will
agree)
I'm proud to be an acorn that has fallen not far from the
tree.

May I Always Remember...

... last hug I got from my mother.

...the excitement of hearing a new Beatles song over the radio for the first time.

... my grandmother's lasagna with the mini meatballs.

... my grandfather teaching me to play "dots."

... the fancy China cup that belonged to my grandmother. After admiring it once, Grandma always gave me that cup to use.

... every dog of mine (especially Freckles).

... the elongated, sky blue balloon with multicolored swirls that my dad gave me when I was a little girl. I always think of that, and him, when I see a sunset.

... my grandfather's clam chowder.
It is the gold standard by which I measure every clam chowder I ever had.

... my husband's love for me.
... God's love for me.

The Tale of the Tape

Muhammad Ali
Is six feet three,
But oh no,
That doesn't bother me.

Muhammad Ali
Weighs two-twenty-four,
But that's not enough,
To send me through the door.

Muhammad Ali
Has lived thirty-three years,
But that's not enough,
To give me any fears.

His chest is forty-four,
His biceps fifteen,
And that's pretty big,
If you know what I mean.

Although on the tale of the tape,
High numbers does he rate,
On a simple IQ test,
He got a seventy-eight.

I'm not afraid to say these things,
You see,
'cause I watch all his fights,
At home on T. V.

Section Poem Backgrounds

The Golden Years

When I was in 10th grade we had a substitute teacher in English class. Our assignment was to write a poem. The teacher said my poem was magnificent and well beyond my years.

This happened shortly after my grandparents' 50th wedding anniversary party. I think that is what inspired the subject.

I never forgot the poem, but thought it was lost forever. Going through some old boxes, there it was!

I am delighted to be able to share with you the thoughts of my teenaged self.

I am...

I don't remember how I got the idea for this one. However, once I started through the alphabet, I had to complete the challenge to find a word beginning with each letter.

Another Birthday
More prose than poetry. An approaching birthday always gets me thinking.

The Loss of a Loved One
For a short period of time, I considered writing greeting cards. This and the next four selections are part of the endeavor.

On Your Wedding Day
For a time, I wrote several versions of this on several wedding cards.

Christmas Ditties
When I was growing up, I liked to make up what I call "Little Ditties". In the case of these, I would write them in the Christmas cards I sent to my family.

I never knew if anyone noticed or liked them until an aunt and uncle celebrated their 25th anniversary. Short on money, I found 25 pennies minted the year they were married and shined them up. Then I wrote a little ditty about the occasion and the fact that the year was the last year the wheat pennies were made. When my aunt opened the present, she excitedly declared that she had gotten one of "Christina's poems."

My Dad

A very short poem about my dad. Although my parents didn't spare the rod and spoil the child, my nine year old self chose these words because they rhyme.

Fancy Pantsy and Roses are Red

When I was 14, one of my teachers gave the class an assignment to write a mini diary. The May 1st entry reads: *I better continue working on my poem book assignment. I'm going to do it real good. Not because I like poetry (so far it has no effect on me whatsoever unless it's mine), but because I feel like going crazy over something.*

I don't know what became of the rest of the assignment, but here are two of the poems I apparently felt were worth keeping.

I Went Down the Falls

Another school assignment. We were writing haikus. This is what I call an extended haiku. However, it has more than three phrases. It has more than 17 beats. It rhymes. Apparently, it isn't a haiku at all.

A Mom's Birthday/A Dad's Birthday

These are birthday card poems for mothers and fathers.

May I Always Remember

Not quite a poem, this is what is called "stream of consciousness." I like this form of writing because it just strings thoughts together and needn't follow the usual rules of punctuation. Having lost loved ones with different forms and degrees of dementia, I couldn't help but think of what I never would want to forget.

The Tale of the Tape

I was in high school when Muhammad Ali was in his second reign as the world heavyweight champion. He was the inspiration for this poem.

Poems I Didn't Write

The poems in this section were written by my husband, Ralph A Walton.

Actual Footage

Distilled
Then contaminated
By points of view
And biased insinuation
What's not shown
Is the preface to the unfolding dramas
The fuel that ignites the response

Android Scream

When love was young and filled the air
I was drenched in hate and sought despair
I pulled the sky down over my eyes
And lived in a world of synthetic compromise

CJD

She's not the woman I first saw
Since I've come to know her
She's so much more

Death Came By

Death came by today
He left the two women and took the man away
Didn't look back, had nothing to say
Came and got what he wanted
And was on his way

Death just stopped on by
He sees opportunity when bullets fly
The young police officer had bad luck on his side
Off duty, in plain clothes, no one realized
He and his gun were silenced in his prime

Sometimes death is in a hurry you see
Slick and smooth ain't in his vocabulary
Now and then it'll happen peacefully
He'll visit us all eventually
And cause us sadness and misery

Nostalgia from a Caveman's Diary

This whole world couldn't be so horrid
This whole world couldn't be so filled with pain
This whole world couldn't be so ugly
Nothing so real could be so insane

Too many people are at odds without reason
I know it happens everywhere I go
How could this world be so ugly
Nothing makes sense and my feeling is low

I've counted the days. I've waited so long
Waited, just waited, for all the world's facts to
      belong
Waited for the last days which seems like a wicked
      dream
Been watching and waiting till all cracks at the
      seams

I don't need no promises
I don't need none of them foolish games
I don't need no one
All their lies are all the same

On Being Born

Enter twilight
Leaving quiet
Was asleep in an ocean
That's now forgotten

Ripe to suffer
Hostile conditions
Surrender silence
Welcome confusion

Been alone
Have grown
Nine months
Been alone

Psychasthenia

Sweet darkness come to erase me
Horror and cruelty come to embrace me
Psychotic fantasy become my lady
Am I the executioner or just a crazy
No guilt, regret is absent
Only another lifeless applicant
Souls bonded, been indentured
I'm just the messenger, behold the intention

When sanity takes a detour
You're in a location of danger
Can only hope for the defender of never
The killer is much too clever

Sweet terror prepare a face for me
Horror and cruelty become our haven of safety
You are well known, and I'm the stranger
There is nothing so exciting as danger
Fatal view of the hunter is delicious
Another victim's end might seem suspicious

The power below has sent for you
My soul has been indentured
There is nothing that gives pleasure like danger
Wouldn't you just love to slice the throat of the
Lone Ranger

Section Poem Backgrounds

I asked my husband, Ralph Walton, if he wanted to give backgrounds to the poems, but he declined. He said the poems speak for themselves.

When I read CJD, I asked if he had another girlfriend with my initials. He said the poem was about me. Just three lines, but I am touched.

Alphabetical Index of Poems

- 108 A Dad's Birthday
- 107 A Mom's Birthday
- 18   A Walking Day
- 118 Actual Footage
- 118 Android Scream
- 98   Another Birthday
- 30   Another Day
- 31   At Last
- 26   Cake Without Frosting is a Muffin
- 102 Christmas Ditties - One thru Three
- 103 Christmas Ditties - Four thru Six
- 104 Christmas Ditties – Seven
- 118 CJD
- 52   Dear Abba

119	Death Came By
10	Ding Dong Belle
32	Epitaph #1
33	Except Jesus
105	Fancy Pantsy
68	God Says
53	He is One of a Kind
96	I am ...
35	I Ask You
75	I Painted Myself
78	I Want to be a Member of the Rich
106	I Went Down a Falls
6	I Won't Go Straight to Heaven
22	Ice Cream
37	I'm Living Because I was Born
63	Imitators of Jesus

55   Jesus is a Loving Savior

65   Jesus' Love

57   Let's Shout His Name

39   Life is a Gift?

90   Limerick #1

90   Limerick #2

91   Limerick #3

92   Limerick #4

92   Limerick #5

92   Limerick #6

86   Loving Luv – A Petrarchan Sonnet

85   Loving Luv - A Shakespearean Sonnet

109   May I Always Remember

105   My Dad

67   My Wish

14   Never Believe a Puppy

120	Nostalgia from a Caveman's Diary
25	Ode to Cheddar Cheese
121	On Being Born
101	On Your Wedding Day
42	Or So I Thought
47	Poor Little Girl
122	Psychasthenia
106	Roses are Red
7	Terri Featherhead
17	The Freckles Song
95	The Golden Years
58	The Lord Sends Rain
100	The Loss of a Loved One
111	The Tale of the Tape
43	The Way that He Tells Me
45	There's a Food in this World

61 We Raise One Voice to You
80 When I Look into the Face - Part One
81 When I Look into the Face - Part Two

Acknowledgements

Many thanks to Steven Porter of Stillwater River Publications for editing the book.

Expressions of gratitude to those who reviewed my book.

Special thanks to my devoted husband, Ralph Walton.

Warm thanks to all who supported and comforted me during my many moods while compiling this book.

Ultimately, all glory goes to God, without whom I would not exist and would not have a promised place to go when I leave this weary world.

Previous Books by Christina J Donato

The Saddest Dog Finds a Friend – eBook and paperback. Available on Amazon.com

The Dog Who Wanted to be Human – eBook and paperback. Available on Amazon.com

My Two Dogs – Their Two Stories – This is a combination of the two above books. It is in paperback. Available at all major online bookstores.

The eBooks are available to read from many public libraries.

About the Author

Christina J Donato was raised on Long Island, NY. She is a graduate of Empire State College, with an AA in Creative Writing and a BA in Political Science & Sociology. She relocated to New England in 1997 for her job as a mainframe programmer. She currently lives in Rhode Island with her husband and their dog, Nera. A proud Baby Boomer, she enjoys word puzzles, black & white movies, anything Beatles, being active in her church, practicing the frame drum, and hosting doggy playdates with Nera.

Social Media

Website:
https://lefthandedauthorpublishing.com/

Facebook Page:
https://www.facebook.com/lhapcjd

Instagram:
christinajdonato

YouTube:
@christinajdonato5029

www.ingramcontent.com/pod-product-compliance
Lightning Source LLC
Chambersburg PA
CBHW060401080526
44583CB00012B/415